S0-BFC-913

101
Ways to Amaze & Entertain

Amazing Magic & Hilarious Jokes to Try on Your Friends & Family

This library edition published in 2017 by Walter Foster Jr.,
an imprint of Quarto Publishing Group USA Inc.
6 Orchard Road, Suite 100
Lake Forest, CA 92630

Cover design by Steve Scott
Page layout by Krista Joy Johnson
Written by Peter Gross and the Walter Foster Jr. Creative Team
Illustrated by Rémy Simard and Brian Biggs

Distributed in the United States and Canada by
Lerner Publisher Services
241 First Avenue North
Minneapolis, MN 55401 U.S.A.
www.lernerbooks.com

First Library Edition

Library of Congress Cataloging-in-Publication Data

Names: Quarto Publishing Limited.
Title: 101 ways to amaze & entertain : amazing magic & hilarious jokes to try
  on your friends & family.
Other titles: One hundred one ways to amaze and entertain | One hundred and
  one ways to amaze and entertain
Description: Lake Forest, CA : Quarto Publishing Group USA Inc., 2016.
Identifiers: LCCN 2016033079 | ISBN 9781942875147 (hardcover)
Subjects: LCSH: Magic tricks. | Card tricks. | Riddles. | Wit and humor.
Classification: LCC GV1547 .A115 2016 | DDC 793.8--dc23
LC record available at https://lccn.loc.gov/2016033079

Printed in USA
9 8 7 6 5 4 3 2 1

101 Ways to Amaze & Entertain

Contents

Card
Tricks

The Key Card

The best card tricks to perform are the ones using a normal pack of cards. The advantage of using a normal pack is that you can perform anywhere, at any time, with any pack of cards.

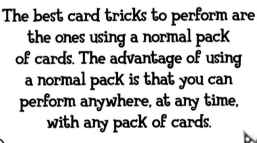

What You Need:
- A pack of cards
- A spectator

This trick is commonly used by all the best magicians to pick out which card a spectator has chosen. The answer is that you must secretly find out which card is on the bottom of the pack.

How to do it:
Step 1 Shuffle the pack of cards as you would normally, and as you straighten the deck, simply take a glance at the bottom card; this is now called the "Key Card."

Step 2 Spread the cards out between both hands, and ask someone to choose one of the cards. Once the card is removed from the deck, close the cards up, and hold the pack in the left hand, as shown in figure A.

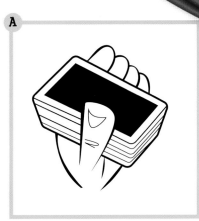

A

Step 3 Ask the spectator to look at the card and remember it.

Step 4 With the right hand, pull out the bottom half of the pack, as shown in figure B, and ask the spectator to place his card on top of the cards in your left hand. Once this has been done, place the cards in your right hand on top of the cards in your left hand. Square up the pack to prove that the chosen card is really lost in the center of the deck.

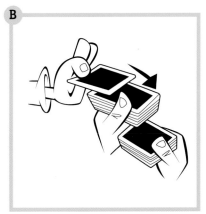

B

Step 5 You placed the Key Card, which was on the bottom of the pack, on top of the chosen card. To find the chosen card, all you need to do is turn the pack faceup and spread it from the left hand to the right. When you see the Key Card, the card to the right of it is the spectator's chosen card. Pull the chosen card out, and amaze your spectator!

Tips from the Pros

You now know the principle of the Key Card. We use it again in the next trick, so don't forget it. When we say, "After a card has been returned to the pack," we mean, "After you have put the Key Card on top of the selected card."

The Next Card

Here is another trick based on the "Key Card." Have a go at dressing it up a little, so picking out the card becomes mysterious, funny, or, best of all, surprising.

What You Need:
- A pack of cards

How to do it:

Step 1 Ask someone to pick a card, and return it as before. Square up the pack, and put it on the table facedown.

Step 2 Now taking cards from the top, put them faceup on the table, one on top of the other, but all crooked. DO NOT put them in a neat pile. Spread them out.

Step 3 As you perform, explain that you will turn over their card in a moment, but if they see it, they mustn't say so.

Step 4 Then, as the cards are turned over, look for the Key Card. Once you come to the Key Card, don't hesitate. You know that the next card will be the selected card. Carry on turning the cards faceup until you have gone two or three cards PAST the selected card, and then stop.

Step 5 "The next card I turn over will be yours," you say. Your spectators know you have passed their card, so the next card cannot be theirs. But they are wrong. Now you reach over to the heap of faceup cards and turn their card facedown. Don't arrange the faceup cards neatly, because you need to see the card to turn it over instantly.

Card Spelling

To prepare the pack, remove the jokers and arrange the cards starting with the aces at the top. Under the aces, put the twos, then the threes, and so on through the pack, ending with the Kings.

What You Need:
- A pack of cards

How to do it:

Step 1 Hold the deck in the left hand and spell the word A-C-E out loud, dealing a card, facedown on the table, for each letter as you spell. Turn the last card of the word faceup and it will be an ace.

Step 2 Now spell the word T-W-O, and repeat the dealing formula, again turning the last card faceup and this card will be a two.

Step 3 Now spell T-H-R-E-E, then F-O-U-R, and so on, right through to the word K-I-N-G, and you will find that every time you turn a card faceup, it will coincide with the word that you are spelling.

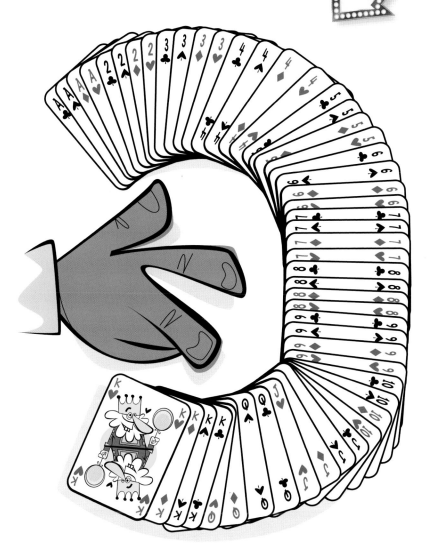

LOL Joke

Q. Why are giraffes so slow
to apologize?

A. It takes them a long time to swallow
their pride.

Foodie Joke

Q. Why do the French like to eat snails?

A. Because they don't like fast food.

Super Silly Joke

Q. What is as big as an elephant but
weighs nothing?

A. Its shadow.

Somersaults

Three cards selected by three different spectators mysteriously reverse themselves in the center of the pack. This is quite a surprising effect and is different from the usual run of card tricks.

What You Need:
- A pack of cards

How to do it:

Step 1 First you must have the three cards selected by three different spectators. As they are removing the cards from the pack, ask them not to look at their cards yet.

Step 2 Once all three cards have been selected, explain that, as you don't wish to get a glimpse of the cards, you are going to turn your back while they look at the cards they have selected.

A

Step 3 Turn your back on the three spectators, turn the pack of cards faceup in your hands, and turn the top card facedown on top of the pack.

Step 4 Now turn back around to face the spectators. Take the card from the first spectator, and push it facedown into the center of the pack, as shown in figure A. Take the second card, and place it facedown in the pack below the first card. Repeat with the third card, pushing it into the pack a little above the first card.

Step 5 Tell them you are going to place the cards behind your back for just a second, and give the pack one complete cut.

Step 6 When you place the pack behind your back, turn the top card faceup, and turn the whole pack over so that it is facedown.

Step 7 Put the pack on the table, and spread out the cards. The three selected cards will be faceup in a facedown pack, as shown in figure B.

B

Tips from the Pros
Don't give the game away by allowing the cards to spread out, showing everyone that it is only the top card which is facedown.

Fingerprints

Another method of picking
out the chosen card
is to pretend that everyone
who takes a card leaves their
fingerprints behind.

What You Need:
- A pack of cards
- A volunteer

How to do it:

Step 1   Ask someone to choose a card and then return it to the deck, placing it underneath your Key Card. Start dealing the cards off the top of the pack, faceup onto the table, looking all the time for fingerprints on the cards. Or so you tell them.

Step 2   As you do so, look for your Key Card. Stop when you turn the Key Card up. You know that the next card is the chosen card.

Step 3   Look at the back of the next card very carefully, and announce that this card is the one with the fingerprints on it. Ask the person to name their chosen card while you turn it over, and, hey presto, there it is, the chosen card! (You just pretend that you can see that person's fingerprints on the card.)

Tips from the Pros

Get the person to name their card before you turn it faceup. It is more theatrical than turning the card over and asking, "Was that your card?"

Super Silly Joke

Q. What is the difference between a car and a bull?

A. A car only has one horn.

Clip-a-Card

The principle is not complicated; just one quick, smooth move of the fingers, and it is done. But it needs confidence and a sure hand, which you get from plenty of practice.

What You Need:

- An ace card
- Two other cards
- A paper clip

How to do it:

Step 1 Place the paper clip on the ace, and place one of the other cards on top of it, as shown in figure A.

Step 2 Hold these two cards in your right hand, thumb on top and first two fingers underneath.

Step 3 Hold the third card in your left hand, thumb on top and first two fingers underneath. Figure B shows the whole setup.

A

B

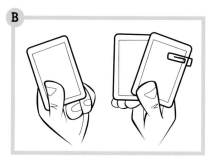

Step 4 Draw attention to the ace with the paper clip on it, and raise both hands to show the faces of the cards, two in the right hand and one in the left hand, as shown in figure C.

Step 5 Now here is the important bit: while lowering your hands, the right thumb and two fingers are swiveled, so that the card under the thumb is slid over to the right, and in doing so the clip is transferred from the lower card to the upper card. This change of position is never noticed, because the clip is still on the edge of the card at that side.

C

Step 6 Lay the three cards out in a row facedown, mix them up, and ask a spectator to pick out the ace.

Step 7 Naturally, they will point to the clipped outer card, but when the card is turned over…amazing…it is not the ace! They will be astonished and are sure to demand that you repeat it. You can do it again by simply replacing the clip on the ace.

Tips from the Pros

If you have trouble transferring the clip, just bend the rounded or pointed inner part of the clip up a little. This will let the edge of the card slide very easily into the clip.

Face-to-Face

This trick doesn't take much, and your friends will be impressed with your magic abilities.

What You Need:
- A pack of cards

How to do it:

Step 1 Shuffle the cards in front of your friend, and then ask him to cut the deck. Tell him to choose one half and put it behind his back, showing him how with the other half saying, "Like this."

Step 2 Ask him to keep the cards behind his back as he chooses a card. Now tell him to look at the card. While he's busy, keep your half behind your back, but turn the bottom card faceup and leave it at the bottom of the deck. Then flip the second card from the top faceup and leave it in the same spot.

A

Step 3 Now tell your friend to place his chosen card facedown on top of his half of the deck and give the whole thing back to you. When he does, place your pile on top of his, and give the deck back to him.

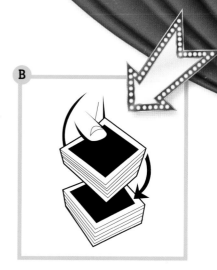

Step 4 Ask him to place the deck behind his back once again and say, "Hocus pocus!" (or whatever your personal magic phrase is) as he takes the top card and puts it at the bottom of the deck.

Step 5 Now turn away and tell your friend to turn the next card faceup. He might say, "Hey, it already IS faceup!"—in which case you act like it's no big deal and say, "Okay, just turn it facedown then."

Step 6 Tell him to insert that card anywhere in the deck and give the deck back to you.

Step 7 Now find the only card in the deck that's faceup—the one right after it is your friend's card!

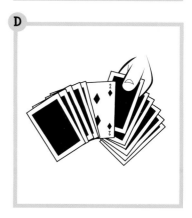

Amazing Fact
Playing cards were invented in China (where paper was invented too) in the year 1120.

Magician's Tip
In "forced" card tricks, messing up the trick before you get it right is done on purpose! If you do the trick too perfectly, it's pretty obvious that you must have known what the card was when your friend picked it. But "messing up" once or twice before you get it right makes people think that you don't know what card they picked, which means that when you actually find it, it must be "magic!"

Amazing Fact
Each King in a deck of playing cards represents a real famous King in history!

Three Strikes

In this trick, you will purposely choose the wrong card twice before choosing the correct one and amazing your friends.

What You Need:
- Paper lunch bag
- Giant Ten of Diamonds Card (template on page 137)
- A pack of cards

How to do it:

Step 1 Make sure the regular ten of diamonds is on top of the deck.

Step 2 Perform the "force" in the "Help Me, I Messed Up" trick on page 30.

Step 3 After you mark the cut, explain that your little league coach taught you how to do a magic trick, but sometimes you need a couple swings before you get a hit: "Don't worry," you say, "three strikes and I'm out."

Step 4 After your friend looks at the card, let him put it back into the deck and shuffle the cards. Then open the paper lunch bag and drop the whole deck in the paper bag. (Be sure that your friend doesn't see the giant ten of diamonds card.)

Step 5 Shake the bag, and hold it up to your ear. Say, "From the sound of the cards, I can tell it was a number card and not a face card, right?"

Step 6 Give the cards another shake, and then open the bag and reach inside without looking. Take out a card and look at it. If it's a jack, queen, or king, say, "I know your card is not a face card, so this is a foul ball." Set the card aside. If it's a number card, show your friend and say, "Was this your card?" When he says "No," yell out, "Strike one!"

Step 7 Keep pulling cards out until you get two strikes. Then before you reach in, say (like a sports announcer), "Well folks, she's got two strikes. The hitter's got to pull something really big out right now to win the game."

Step 8 Reach into the bag, and pull out the giant ten of diamonds. "Was this your card?" Your victim will be amazed!

You Pick

Convince your friend that they are also a magician in this trick.

What You Need:
- A pack of cards

How to do it:

Step 1 Tell your friend you think she has a gift for magic too. This trick will prove it! Shuffle the cards, and casually get a look at the bottom card. (For example, let's say it's the king of clubs.)

Step 2 Spread the cards out on a table, facedown. Tell your friend to concentrate really hard, and ask her to point to the king of clubs.

A

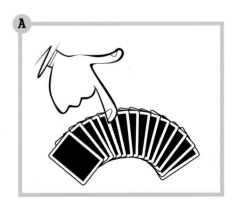

Step 3 Take the card that she points to out of the deck (but don't let her see it). Let's say it's the five of hearts. Look intrigued, and say, "Hmmmm..."

Step 4 Now ask her to point to the five of hearts. Pick that card up without showing it to her (we'll pretend it's the ten of spades). Look surprised and say, "Wow! Now I'll pick a card."

Step 5 Say the name of the last card your friend picked (for example, "I'm looking for the ten of spades!")

Step 6 Pick up the bottom card (your original card). Now you'll have three cards in your hand.

Step 7 Squint and look mysteriously at your friend while you mix up the three cards in your hand—then show them to her and exclaim, "You're amazing! What else can you do?"

B

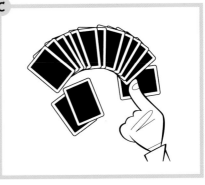

C

Step 8 If, by some weird twist of fate, your friend picks the bottom card at some point, it's okay! Just show her the cards she's chosen, and tell her she has incredible ESP.

Help Me, I Messed Up!

Who says the Web is a waste of time? After having the worst time figuring out what card your friend is thinking of, you reach into your pocket and show her the website where you learned this trick. When she punches in the address, she gets a website that reads her mind!

What You Need:
- A pack of cards
- Junior Magician Card (template on page 141)

This trick may reveal the biggest secret in this whole book—if this doesn't impress you, go back and read it again! This is bigger than any alien landing coverup or any international conspiracy. This is a bigger secret than the president being a robot. (You knew that, right?) Okay, here it is...magicians have ways of making you pick a certain card even when you think you are getting a free choice—it's the "force!" Huge, huh?

Pre-performance prep:
Make sure the three of hearts is on top of the deck. You can use any card in the force, but for this trick you will make your friend pick the three of hearts.

How to do it:

Step 1 To start, shuffle the cards, but make sure you don't change the top card. Try this: Hold the cards faceup; then grab some cards from the middle of the deck, and toss them on the bottom of the deck. Do this a couple of times before you start; that way no one will accuse you of having the cards in order.

Step 2 Place the deck on the table. Tell your friend to cut the deck in half, and place the two piles of cards on the table. Say, "I'm going to take this half and put it on top to mark the cut." Pick up the bottom half of the deck, and place it sideways across the top half, forming a cross with the two halves. (The three of hearts will be the top card on the bottom half of the deck.)

Step 3 Now it's time to distract your audience from the cards. Take out your Junior Magician Card, and explain how you found this great magic book that included this card, so you never have to worry about messing up a trick. This is a very important step: You are about to do something very sneaky, and you need your audience to focus on something other than the cards, even for just a couple of seconds.

Step 4 Put down the Junior Magician Card, and pick up the top half of the cards. With your index finger, point at the top card of the bottom half of the deck and say, "Okay, now take a look at the card you cut to."

A

Shuffle the deck without changing the top card.

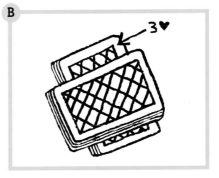
B

Form a cross with the cut cards.

C

Hold half of the deck, and point at the top card.

Step 5 Ask your friend to look at the card, and then replace it anywhere into the deck. Tell her, to be really honest, you will turn your head while she replaces the card.

Choose the wrong card on purpose.

Go to the website.

Step 6 Put the two halves of the deck together, and then spread out all the cards on the table. Move your hands mysteriously over the cards, and then turn one over. Announce, "This is your card!" Your friend will inform you that you are wrong. Do it again, picking another wrong card.

Step 7 Pretend to get really frustrated. Then pick up the Junior Magician Card, and show your friend the website listed: http://quartoknows.com/page/help-i-messed-up

Step 8 Take your friend to the nearest computer, and log on to the Internet. Go to the site, and let your friend answer the meaningless questions. Then make sure she clicks the "Analyze" button. The website will flash the name of the correct card—the three of hearts—and your friend won't believe her eyes!

More Help Me, I Messed Up!

Extra stuff to know and think about:

If you want to do the trick, but you can't get on the Internet, check this out: On the back of the of the Junior Magician Card it says, "Void where prohibited. This offer exempt in the Galápagos Islands and some parts of Madagascar. By the way, your friend picked the three of hearts, so don't blame us if you can't do the trick."

Dice
Tricks

Dicey Dice

The interesting part of this effect is that at a certain point you ask the spectator to watch your hand to see that there are no funny moves. At that moment, there are no funny moves. The "funny move" was performed the first time you moved your hand.

What You Need:
- A die

A

How to do it:

Step 1 Hold a die between the first finger and thumb of the right hand, as shown in figure A, showing the number 6. There is a 6 at the front, a 1 at the back, and a 3 on top.

Step 2 Now, as you turn the right hand over to show the number on the other side, roll the die between your finger and thumb, as shown in figure B, so that the 3 is showing.

Step 3 Now reverse the action; turn your hand back and roll the die again so it is showing a 6. With the die back in the same position as at the start, ask a spectator if they can remember the number on the other side of the die. They will naturally say "3."

Step 4 Now ask them to watch your hand to make sure there are no funny moves. Very slowly, turn your right hand over, and the spectator will be amazed to see that there is a 1 on the other side of the die.

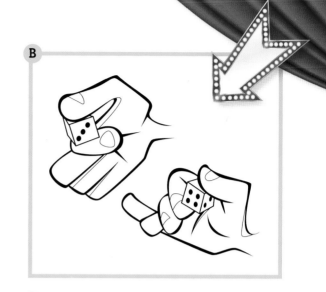

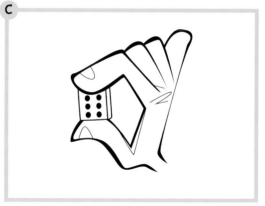

Magician's Tip
Have confidence in yourself! If you seem unsure, your audience may get bored.

The Magic Number

Your friends will
think you have awesome
magic skills with this trick!

What You Need:
- Three dice

How to do it:

Step 1 Here's the deal—you probably didn't know this, but the opposite sides of a die always add up to seven. If a 1 is on top, a 6 will be on the bottom; if a 2 is on top, a 5 will be on the bottom— get the idea?

Step 2 Pass the dice around so your friends can see that they're real.

A

Step 3 Tell your friends that even though the dice look solid, they are transparent to you. You can see right through them to the other side. Ask someone to roll the dice on a table.

Step 4 Ask for complete silence for the sake of your total concentration. Wave your hand (or wand) over the dice, whispering some magical-sounding words ("Abracadabra" is a good one).

Step 5 Now turn the dice over, one at a time, saying the number as you go. Your friends are bound to be impressed!

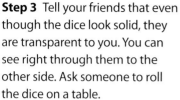

Magical Addition

Guessing a total without
seeing the figures
always impresses an audience.
So try this trick.

What You Need:
- Three dice

How to do it:

Step 1 Explain to the audience that you want them to throw three dice on the table and push all three together while your back is turned.

Step 2 When they have done this, and while your back is still turned, ask them to add all three numbers together.

Step 3 When they tell you they have done this, instruct them to add the three numbers on the bottom of the dice to the first three numbers, and then tell them to place all three dice in their pocket so you cannot possibly see them.

Step 4 Once all your instructions have been carried out, turn to face them, write something on a piece of paper, and place it on the table. Ask them to tell you the total of all the numbers they added together. They will say "21."

Step 5 Ask them to read what you wrote on the piece of paper. When they read it, it says, "I PREDICT THE TOTAL WILL BE 21."

Step 6 This works because the two opposite sides of a die always add up to seven, so the opposite sides of three dice will always add up to 21.

Super Silly Joke
Q. What do you do if your dog chews a dictionary?
A. Take the words out of his mouth.

LOL Joke
Two atoms are walking the road. One says, "I think I lost an electron." The other says, "Are you sure?" The first one says, "I'm positive."

Amazing Fact
Ancient Greeks made their dice out of sheep ankle bones.

LOL Joke
Q. Did you hear about the dog that went to the flea circus?
A. He stole the show.

Amazing Fact
The first product the Nintendo Company ever sold was playing cards, more than 100 years ago!

Super Silly Joke
Q. Why did the elephant leave the circus?
A. He was tired of working for peanuts.

The "Under 21" Prediction

Another presentation uses exactly the same principle, but although you use three dice as in the previous trick, the total is not 21. You proceed as follows.

What You Need:
- Three dice

How to do it:

Step 1 Ask the audience to throw three dice on the table while your back is turned.

Step 2 When they have done this, instruct them to stack the three dice one on top of the other.

Step 3 Now turn around and point out that although you can see the dice, there are a number of sides that you can't see. There are in fact five sides of the dice that you can't see.

Step 4 Turn your back again, and instruct them to add all the hidden numbers up to make one total.

Step 5 When they have done this, ask them to place all three dice in your hand, which you are holding behind your back.

Step 6 Then turn to face them, still holding the dice behind your back.

Step 7 Explain that simply by a sense of touch you know that the total was 21, and of course you are correct.

Step 8 As before, the tops and bottoms of all three dice still add up to 21. All you do is subtract the number on top of the uppermost die (which is a 3) from 21, which gives you 18.

The Inertia Trick

This is one of those little stunts which looks as if it can't be done. But it can! The challenge is to remove the coin from under the dice without ever touching or moving the dice away from the coin.

What You Need:
- Three or four dice
- Two coins

How to do it:

Step 1 First stack three or four dice on top of a coin. Now ask a spectator if they can remove the coin, without touching the dice and leaving them stacked as they are.

Step 2 When the spectator gives in, take another coin and place it on the table about 6 inches away from the stack of dice.

Step 3 Place your forefinger firmly on this coin and, sliding it across the table, strike the other coin, which will push it out from under the dice, leaving them exactly as they are.

LOL Joke

Two cannibals are eating a clown. One turns to the other and says, "Does this taste funny to you?"

Super Silly Joke

Q. What stays in the corner and travels all over the world?

A. A stamp.

The Color-Changing Die

For this trick, photocopy and assemble the magic die template on page 143. When you perform this trick, make sure you don't get too excited and crush your die! No matter how you look at a die, you can only see three sides at time. This particular die can appear to be either green, blue, and purple or white, according to the angle from which you look at it.

What You Need:
- Magic Die Template (template on page 143)
- Glue

How to do it:
Step 1 Place the die on your left palm.

A

Step 2 Place your right palm on top of it, and roll the die forward on the left palm until the other three sides are facing your spectator.

Step 3 Raise your right hand, and the die will appear to have changed color.

Step 4 If you reverse the action, the die will change back to its original color.

B

C

Super Silly Joke
Q. How do you know when the moon has had enough to eat?
A. When it's full.

Amazing Fact
The dots on a die are called "pips."

Hand
Tricks

Ring 'n' Rope

This is a cross between a magic trick and a juggling stunt. Tie a knot in a piece of rope, thread a gold ring through the end, give it a toss, and magically it lands in the center of the knot.

What You Need:
- A rope (or piece of ribbon)
- A ring

How to do it:

Step 1   Tie a loose knot in the middle of the rope, and then thread the ring onto it.

Step 2   Toss the ring through the loop in a downward motion to make sure that it will land in the center of the knot.

Step 3   As the ring lands in the loop, pull your hands apart, tightening the knot a little and enclosing the ring in it.

Tips from the Pros
For this trick, you can use almost anything that is ring-shaped: a metal nut, a washer, even an old-fashioned bottle opener.

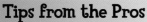

Amazing Fact
In India, playing cards are round.

Foodie Joke
Q. What's the best thing to put in a pie?
A. Your teeth.

Watch That Ring

This is a slightly spooky effect. A ring is placed on a rubber band stretched flat. Very slowly, the ring seems to move itself along the rubber band from one end to the other.

What You Need:
- A ring
- A long, thin rubber band

How to do it:

Step 1 The method is both simple and very subtle. Hold the rubber band between the forefinger and thumb of each hand. Be sure to leave an extra bit of elastic at each end, although the middle part between the hands should be stretched fully.

Step 2 Tip the ring to one end, so it touches the left finger and thumb.

Step 3 Now, ever so slightly, relax your grip on the band with the left finger and thumb. The tightness of the stretched band will pull the extra elastic from the left, making the rubber band move. The ring, which is hanging from the rubber band, will move with it.

Step 4 Now relax the right finger and thumb. The ring will appear to move back in the opposite direction!

Magician's Tip
When you're practicing your tricks, don't forget to rehearse what you'll be saying too. What you say is just as important as what you do!

Magic Mending

· · · · · · · · · · · · · · · · · · · ★ ·

This is surprisingly one of the simplest
magic tricks to perform. Put a length
of ribbon through a paper tube. With the ends
of the ribbon showing, take a pair of scissors
and cut through the paper tube containing
the ribbon. Now pull the ribbon
free of the paper tube, showing
the ribbon amazingly
untouched and in one piece.

What You Need:

- A pair of scissors
- 18 inches of ribbon
- An envelope

How to do it:

Step 1 To prepare this trick, make a tube out of an ordinary envelope by sealing it and cutting a strip off both ends. Then cut a slot slightly bigger than the ribbon in the back of the envelope. Slip the ribbon through, an end showing at each end of the tube, and push a little loop out through the slot. Now you are ready to perform.

Step 2 Hold the envelope in the left hand, the slotted side facing down, hidden. Slip the pointed end of the scissors under the tube, with the ribbon pulled slightly through the slot. (The scissors slip between the ribbon and the envelope, as shown in figure A.)

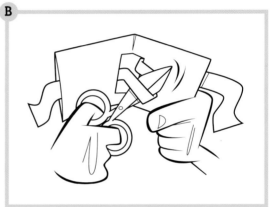

Step 3 Fold the tube over the bottom blade of the scissors with your left hand, and cut the envelope, as shown in figures B and C.

Step 4 Straighten the envelope, hold it in your left hand, and pull the ribbon free.

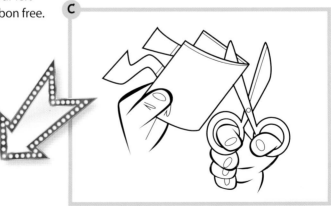

Ribbon Release

The cutting and restoring of a piece of rope is a trick which dates back several hundred years, and since then, magicians have been devising all kinds of other tricks with rope, string, and ribbon. Ribbon is often used because it is more colorful, smoother, and more theatrical. String is the great standby of the "close-up" magician.

What You Need:
- 20 inches of ribbon
- A spectator's buttonhole

How to do it:

Step 1 Tie the ends of the ribbon together to form a loop. When you are ready, pick up the loop of ribbon, slip it through the buttonhole, and then put it over your left-hand forefinger and over your right-hand middle finger.

A

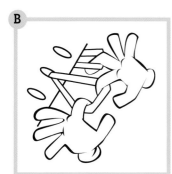

B

Step 2 Bring both hands together, and unnoticed by the spectator, slip the right forefinger into the left loop of ribbon, thumb on top, first two fingers underneath.

Step 3 Two things now happen at the same time. Quickly take the right middle finger out of the right loop of ribbon, leaving the two forefingers in the left loop. Pull the two hands apart. The ribbon will now be free of the buttonhole. It all happens so fast that the audience cannot follow what happened. It actually looks as if the ribbon has in some weird and wonderful way ripped through the cloth without tearing anything.

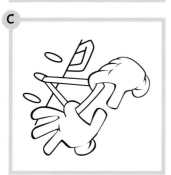

C

Tips from the Pros

This effect works best with ribbon, but it can be performed with string. Experience has taught the magical brotherhood that ribbon is smoother, so we recommend it.

Note the position of the knotted ends of the ribbon, and the left side of the loop. This ensures that the knot isn't pulled through the buttonhole with a jerk.

Magician's Tip

If you do mess up a trick for real, don't tell your audience. If you play it off well, they'll never even know!

Super Silly Joke

Q. What do you call a spider with no legs?
A. A raisin.

LOL Joke

Q. When is a baseball player like a spider?
A. When he catches a fly.

Amazing Fact

A human stomach can stretch to hold more than a quart of food.

When Is a Cut Not a Cut?

• • • • • • • • • • • • • • • ⭐ • • • • • • • • • • • • • •

This is another trick to make
the spectators doubt their own eyes.
They see a string cut, and a moment
later it appears not in two pieces as
they expected, but still as one.
How did it happen? Well, read on.

What You Need:
- About 3 feet of string (or ribbon)
- A pocket of your own
- A spectator

How to do it:

Step 1 Take some string, and tie it in a loop.

Step 2 Now loop it through itself as shown in figure A. Hold both ends of the loop and the knot in the left hand, hiding the way it is looped over itself.

Step 3 Ask a spectator to cut through both strings, as shown in figure B.

Step 4 Let go with the right hand, and with your left hand, put the two pieces in your pocket.

Step 5 Ask two spectators to each take hold of one end of the string hanging from your pocket. As the string emerges from your pocket, it seems to have been restored to one long piece, just as if it had never been cut. The short piece containing the knot is left behind in your pocket.

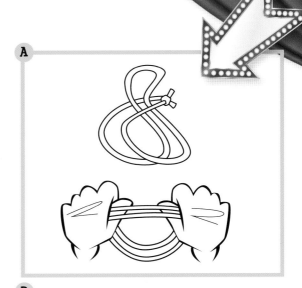

A

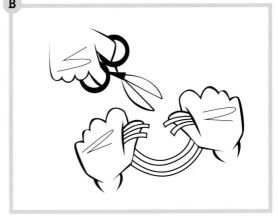

B

Super Silly Joke

Q. Why did the golfer need an extra pair of pants?

A. So he could get a hole in one.

A Knotty Problem

This is a nice little trick that includes your audience in the fun. Hand a piece of rope to a spectator, and ask if she can tie a knot in the rope without ever releasing the ends, which, of course, they cannot possibly do however much they wriggle.

What You Need:
- A rope (or piece of ribbon)

How to do it:
Step 1 Put one end of the rope firmly into each of your spectator's hands, as shown in figure A, and ask them to tie a knot. The important thing is that they have to do it without ever letting go of the rope.

A

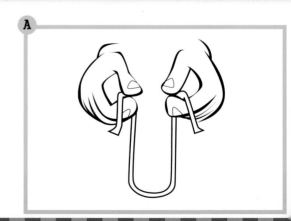

Step 2 When they admit they can't do it, take the rope from their hands, passing the right hand in front of the rope to take the left-hand end, and the left hand behind the rope in front of the right hand to take the right-hand end, as shown in figure B.

Step 3 As you separate your arms, presto, a knot will form itself in the rope!

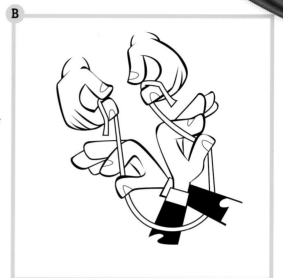

Tips from the Pros

Remember to put one end of the rope into each of the spectator's hands, as shown in figure A. If allowed to put it down, it is possible to tie a knot, so if they try to, explain that they may not let go.

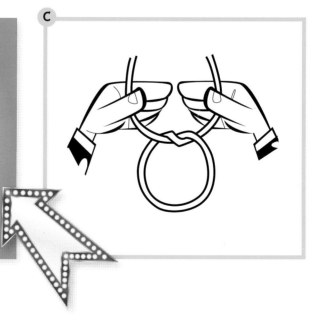

Finger Fun

This is a stand-by of the magician
who likes to perform close to his audience.
Tricks done up close, rather than from
a stage or area set apart, have become very popular
with magicians. They move around performing among
the audience, which requires a specific
group of tricks, none relying on hiding
behind something else. This trick
makes a rubber band, placed on two
fingers, seem to jump across
to the other fingers for no reason at all.

What You Need:
- A rubber band
- Your hand

How to do it:

Step 1 The trick is in the secret action of the left thumb. Place the band on the two fingers of the left hand, as shown in figure A.

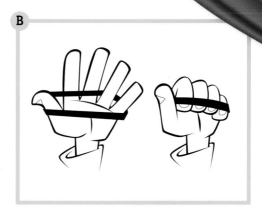

Step 2 Now turn the hand, its back away from you, and insert the left thumb under the rubber band as you close it into a fist. This stretches it while you insert the tips of all four fingers under the rubber band.

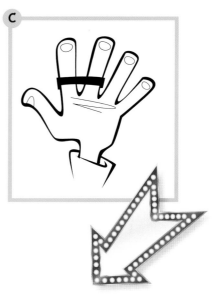

Step 3 The action of straightening the fingers out will cause the outer end of the rubber band to slip over the fingertips from one pair of fingers to the other. It happens so fast that the eye cannot follow, and it looks as if the rubber band has jumped from one pair of fingers to the other, as shown in figure C.

Super Silly Joke
Q. What do you call a fly with no wings?
A. A walk.

Riddle-
Me-Ring

Intertwine a rubber band around the fingers of your right hand. Borrow a ring from someone's finger. Hold the ring in the left hand, and hold the right hand up, palm toward the spectator. Now, very quickly, put the ring on the middle finger of the right hand, seeming to actually penetrate the rubber band.

What You Need:
- A rubber band
- A ring

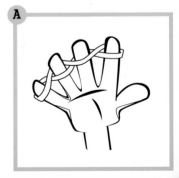

How to do it:

Step 1 Place the rubber band on the right fingers, as shown in figure A.

Step 2 Hold your left hand out to take the ring from a spectator, and as you do, casually drop your right hand to your side.

A

Step 3 As you drop your right hand, withdraw the middle finger from within the rubber band, and place it so that the two strips of the band are in front of your finger, as shown in figure B.

Step 4 Hold the right hand up again as before, and drop the ring onto your finger.

Step 5 It must be done quickly, and as soon as the ring is on your finger, pull the rubber band off your hand, and return the ring to the lender.

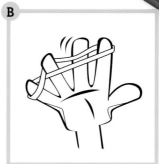

B

C

A Magic Release

This illusion is a real teaser. The trick is in what you say to your friends when explaining what to do. They must hold a rubber band with fingers and thumbs together and then let it go while their fingers and thumbs are still touching.

What You Need:
- A rubber band
- A friend

How to do it:

Step 1 Hold a rubber band in two places, between the thumb and forefinger of each hand, as shown in figure A. Tell your friends that they have to hold the rubber band in this way.

Step 2 When they have done this, ask them to release the rubber band, but their fingers and thumbs must remain touching at all times.

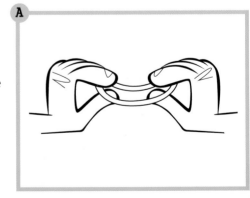

A

Step 3 To show them how, do the same, but then bring your hands together so that the tips of the forefingers are touching and the tips of the thumbs are touching.

Step 4 Now separate the fingers as shown in figure B, and the rubber band will drop to the floor. Bingo!

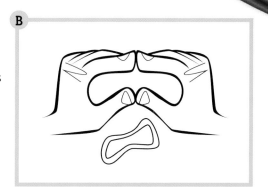

Foodie Joke

Q. What's a light-year?

A. It's just like a regular year, but with fewer calories.

Super Silly Joke

Q. What has one head, one foot, and four legs?

A. A bed.

Amazing Fact

The words *hocus-pocus* come from a Norse fairy-tale wizard, Ochus Bochus.

LOL Joke

Q. Why does a flamingo stand on one leg?

A. Because if he lifted the other leg, he would fall down.

Super Silly Joke

Q. Why was the math book sad?

A. It had too many problems.

Where Is It Now?

This is an excellent vanishing trick. Put a coin in the center of an ordinary pocket handkerchief. Shake the handkerchief out—where did that coin go?

What You Need:
- A coin
- A pocket handkerchief
- A rubber band

A

How to do it:

Step 1 The secret is simple: a rubber band. Secretly put the band over the thumb and first two fingers of the left hand, as shown in figure A. Then drape a pocket handkerchief over the left hand.

Step 2 Push a coin down into the center of the handkerchief. Without the spectators knowing, you are actually pushing it inside the ring made by the rubber band.

Step 3 Bring the left fingertips and thumb together, and the rubber band will slip over them and trap the coin in the handkerchief.

Step 4 Now take a corner with your right hand, and sharply pull the handkerchief away and shake it. The coin is trapped by the band; it cannot fall out, so the spectators think that it has disappeared.

B

Tips from the Pros

If the only rubber band available is too large, just double it over, so it goes around the fingers and thumb twice.

Ring-a-Ring-a-String

This is a true classic of magic—a trick
that is at least 150 years old!
The instructions may seem a little
confusing, but pay attention to whose right
and left the instructions talk about and
you should have no problem.

What You Need:
- A piece of string (or ribbon)
- A ring

How to do it:

Step 1 Tie the string into a loop.

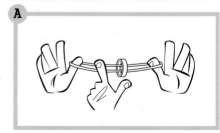

A

Step 2 Now thread the ring onto the loop of
string, and slip the string over a spectator's
thumbs. Figure A shows the setup.

Step 3 To remove the ring from the string, put your left forefinger on both strings,
as shown in figure A. With the right first finger and thumb, pick up a single strand
of string. Now, without removing your left forefinger, pull the strand of string across
and loop it over the spectator's right thumb, as shown in figure B.

B

Step 4 Push the ring to the left as far as possible. Now pick up the same single string, and loop this over the same right thumb, as shown in figure C. During all this, your left forefinger must remain on both strings.

C

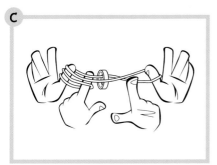

Step 5 Now instruct the spectator to touch the tips of his forefingers to the tips of his thumbs, ensuring that the loops cannot slip over the thumbs.

Step 6 All you have to do is remove your left forefinger with a flourish from the strings, and presto, the ring will release itself from the string.

Holey String!

The ring and the string are solid, so how can you pop the ring on and off the center of the string? These are two amazing stunts that your friends will never figure out!

What You Need:

- Ring and string (or ribbon)
- A story like this to tell: *A long time ago, a king had a valuable ring, and he was afraid that a thief would steal it. To protect the ring, the king threaded it on a string so the thief would have to sneak it off to steal it. But once it was on the string, the king realized he had a bigger problem: Instead of having one ring to protect, he had two ends of the string to watch. He crossed the ends and put a guard right where the string crossed itself. But the thief knew magic and was still able to steal the ring!*

How to do it:

Step 1 Thread the string through the ring, and place the ring in the center of your palm, with the string hanging off each side. Mention that the only way the ring can come off the string is if it slides off one of the two ends. Say, "I will cross the ends so there is only one point to watch: the place where they overlap."

Hold the string and ring in your hand like this.

Step 2 Close your hand around the ring, and turn it palm down. With your other fist, grab the string with your thumb and index finger, and slide it down to the end as you drape the string over the back of your hand.

Step 3 Grab the other end of the string, but as you do, rotate your ring hand so your thumb is up and your pinkie is down. Then loosen your fist to let the ring fall into your waiting hand. Close your hand around the ring, and slide your thumb and index finger down to the end of the string. Drape the string over the back of your right hand, forming an X.

Step 4 Have your friend place his finger on the center of the string as you say, "Now there is no way for the ring to get loose without you seeing it, right?" Place your other fist under this one, and rub your hands together mysteriously. Then bring your free hand out and show that the ring has "melted" through the center of the string and into your other hand!

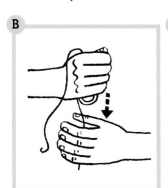

B

Slide your hand down one end of string, and drape it over your hand.

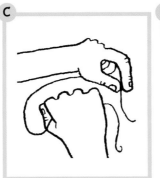

C

Drop the ring into your hand while draping the other end of the string.

D

Rub both of your fists together mysteriously.

More Holey String Fun

If your friend wants you to do it again,
do this trick instead:

Step 1 Have your friend hold one end of the string down against a table, while you hold the other end.

Step 2 Hold the string taut, thread it through the ring, and hold the ring in the center of the string.

Step 3 Pull the ring to the side just a bit, and give the ring a single turn. The string ends up twisted around the ring.

Step 4 Say, "To make this twice as hard, I will loop the ring twice." Rotate the ring so the loop is at the bottom.

Step 5 Take the end you are holding, and loop it back through the ring, so the ring looks like figure D and not like figure C.

Step 6 Make sure your friend can see the ring on the string, and loosen the string just a little (give it some slack). Grip the ring on the right side and pull. The ring will pop off the center of the string!

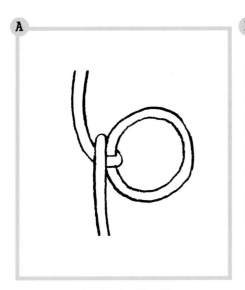

Twist the ring like this.

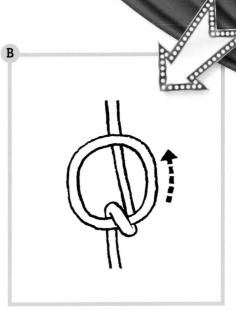

Now rotate it like this.

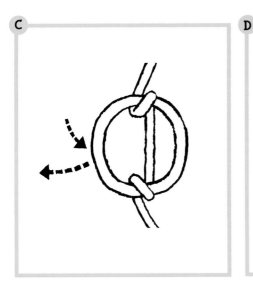

Don't loop your end like this . . .

. . . loop it so it looks like this.
Then pull the ring off.

Practical Jokes & Pranks

Airmail Rattlesnake

Braaaack! Made of bent wire, a rubber band, and a metal ring, this homemade noisemaker fits neatly in an envelope until it is opened. You can even send it through the mail!

What You Need:

- One heavy-gauge paper clip
- A couple of small rubber bands
- A metal washer with a diameter of about 1¼ inches (From your local hardware store)
- A medium-sized, heavy-paper envelope

How to do it:

Step 1 Form your paper clip into the shape shown in figure A. Pick out two rubber bands that are each about half the length of the wire. If the rubber bands are too big, the rattlesnake won't work. Thread each rubber band through the ring and then through itself, so that it looks like figure B.

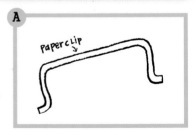

A

paper clip

Bend the paper clip so that it looks like this.

Step 2 Loop the rubber bands around the "hooks" on the end of the wire as shown in figure C. Hold the paper clip, and with your other hand, spin the ring so that the two rubber bands twist. Keep turning: The more you turn it, the more "sensitive" the rattlesnake will be. (Stop if you see the wire bending too much.)

Step 3 Reposition the whole thing in one hand. Without letting the rubber bands untwist, place the contraption deep into the envelope, and close the flap. The closed envelope will keep the "rattlesnake" from spinning. See figure D.

Step 4 Just for fun, open up the envelope. If everything is set up right, opening the envelope should make the washer spin and hit the sides of the envelope, making an obnoxiously loud noise. If it didn't work, you may need to position the rattlesnake a little differently in the envelope. After a couple of tries, you'll figure out how to make it work reliably.

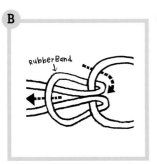

B

Thread your rubber bands through the washer as shown on each side.

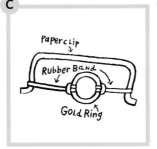

C

Make the wire, rubber bands, and ring look like this. Then twist the ring to wind it up.

D

Place the wire and twisted rubber band contraption into the envelope.

More Rattlesnake Fun

The rattlesnake can be used one of two ways—live or left as a booby trap. Here are some suggestions:

- **Leave it on top of a pile of books on the kitchen table.** Go in the other room and wait for your mom to notice it.

- **Put it in your lunch box.** At lunch, take it out, and hold the rattler from untwisting while you look into the envelope. Say, "Wow, cool!" and then close it and put it down. Someone is bound to ask what it is. Tell them it's hard to explain, but they can take a look if they want to...

- **And the best:** Put the envelope into a bigger envelope and mail it to a friend. Write a note on the envelope that says, "I know you're going to love this, but it's a little hard to put together. Give me a call and I'll talk you through it, but wait until we are on the phone before you open it. The pieces can easily get lost if you're not careful." This way you can hear them scream over the phone. They'll never see it coming!

Wet-Penny
Basketball

Show your friend a new game: Take a penny, wet it,
and stick it to your forehead. After you count to five,
wrinkle your forehead and the penny drops right
into your glass. Then let your friend
try. Try to hold back the laughter
while she wrinkles and squirms.
Why won't that penny drop?!

What You Need:

- A glass of cold water, without ice
- A penny

How to do it:

Step 1 Tell your friends that you will show them how to play a new game of skill.
Take the penny, dip it into the water, and then tip your head back—eyes closed—
and place the penny on the center of your forehead. Now say, "One, two, three—let's
play wet-penny basketball!"

Step 2 Slowly tip your head forward and move your eyebrows up and down until the penny falls off your forehead and (hopefully) into the glass.

Hold your head back, eyes closed, and place a wet penny on your forehead.

Step 3 Offer to let one of your friends try the game. Reach into the glass, and take out the penny. Tell your friend to tilt her head back and close her eyes while you put the penny on her forehead. When you reach out with the penny, let it drop from your fingertips into your closed hand. Instead of putting the penny on her forehead, just push your cold wet finger on her forehead. Because of the water and the temperature of your finger, she will "feel" the penny on her forehead.

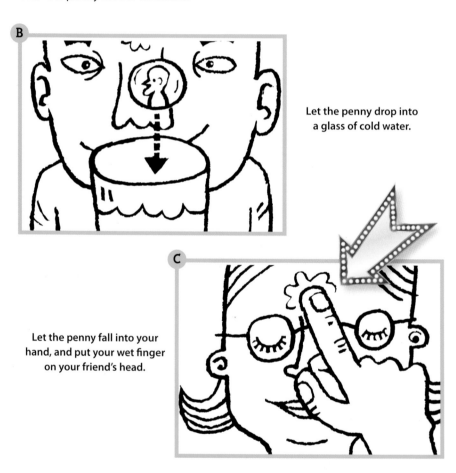

Let the penny drop into a glass of cold water.

Let the penny fall into your hand, and put your wet finger on your friend's head.

Step 4 Now sit back and watch! After counting, she will tilt forward and start moving her eyebrows to try to make the penny drop. If she seems confused, encourage her to keep going by saying, "Oh, it's stuck! Keep going; it's about to drop!" Once you've had your fun, tell her to reach up and take the penny off her head. When she reaches up and finds no penny, open your hand and tell her she wins anyway. Tee-hee!

Extra stuff to know and think about:

Okay, I admit this is kind of mean. But no one gets hurt, and trust me—once you catch people with this trick, they will want to turn around and do it to someone else. So stop feeling guilty and get to work!

Empty Head

Prove to your friends that you've got plenty of room in there. Stick your finger in your ear—your cheek puffs out! Pour milk into your ear—it comes out your mouth! If you do this just right, your friend may prove that milk can go in his mouth—and come out his nose!

This is a must-know for all class clowns; it's what's known in the magic world as a "quickie." This isn't so amazing that the local newspaper is going to call you, but—if done right— you will get a big laugh in the lunchroom. And isn't that what life is all about?

What You Need:
- A drink in a can or carton (This works best with a drink in a non-see-through container. On the other hand, the whole thing works mostly on good coordination and shock value, so you could probably get away with using any drink, once you know how to do it smoothly.)
- Your tongue—the big, fleshy muscle in your mouth

How to do it:

Step 1 Take a sip of your tasty beverage, and leave it in your mouth without swallowing.

Step 2 With your fingers curled into a loose fist, reach up and stick your index finger in your ear.

Step 3 As your finger goes in your ear, move your tongue against the opposite cheek. This makes it look as if your finger is going through your head and across your mouth. It doesn't look totally real, but it does look cool! To heighten the illusion, move your finger up and down (like you're scratching) at the same time that you move your tongue up and down against your cheek.

Step 4 Take your finger out of your ear, and lift your drink up to your ear. Tilt it slightly to create the illusion of pouring, and spit out your mouthful of drink in a beautifully aimed arch! A messy gag, but very entertaining!

Extra stuff to know and think about:

Do not push your finger into your ear and actually try to make it come out your mouth. It is impossible—and it hurts. Do not actually pour milk (or any other drink) into your ear either. It may not hurt, but you will look silly with milk in your ear.

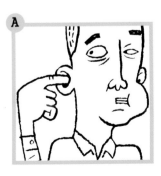

A

With your finger in your ear, push your tongue against your cheek.

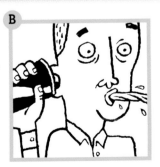

B

Pretend to pour in your ear, and spit out liquid at the victim.

LOL Joke

A horse walks into the school yard, and the teacher asks, "So why the long face?"

Super Silly Joke

Q: What do you call a sheep with no legs?
A: A cloud.

LOL Joke

Q. What do you get from a pampered cow?
A. Spoiled milk.

Super Silly Joke

Q. What did the pencil say to the other pencil?
A. You're looking sharp.

Smell-a-Vision

Do people say you smell? Well, prove that you do!
With just a whiff, you can tell whose
stinky sock is whose. Only the nose knows!

What You Need:
- Four medium-sized plastic freezer bags (Get the kind with the white printing on them.)
- A pencil eraser
- A container large enough to hold all four bags (A large paper bag from the supermarket or a small, clean garbage can would be perfect.)

Pre-performance prep:

The best place to do this trick is around your kitchen or dining room table—or someplace where your friends can easily take off one shoe and sock but you can't see what their socks look like. To make this trick work, you need to mark each bag by erasing small parts of the white printing off the bags. You don't have to do much— once you know what you're looking for, it will be easy to see even the smallest mark. Keep the bags in the kitchen until you're ready to do the trick.

Bag 1: Erase top left corner

Bag 2: Erase top right corner

Bag 3: Erase top right and left corners

Bag 4: Erase nothing

How to do it:

Step 1 Tell your friends about your special ability to detect their distinct odors, and suggest that they help you with an experiment. As you go to the kitchen to get your four freezer bags, take a second to alphabetize your friends (don't worry, this quick brain activity won't leave a scar). For example, if your friends are Ruth, Dave, Arlo, and Kristin, mentally put them in alphabetical order: Arlo (1), Dave (2), Kristin (3), Ruth (4). Now make sure the bags are in the same order: 1, 2, 3, 4. That's the way you'll hand them out.

Have a friend put their socks into the fixed bag.

Step 2 Go back to your friends, hand out the bags, and tell them to take off one sock and place it in the bag. Tell them that the separate bags will keep the odors from mixing. Since you don't want to see what their socks look like, turn your back and tell them that once they take their socks off, it's very important to get the socks into the bags and seal them quickly. This will keep "their unique odors from mixing with the other sock smells."

B

Dramatically sniff the sock
in each bag.

C

LOOK at
LABeL

Peek inside each bag, and look at
the erased corners.

Step 3 If you are all sitting around a table, have everyone hand the bags under the table to one of your friends, who puts them into the container. If you aren't around a table, have everyone place his or her bag into the container while your back is still turned so you can't see whose sock is whose.

Step 4 Close the top of the container, and give it a shake. Make sure that everyone agrees that the socks are mixed and that you will have only your sense of smell to help you determine whose sock is whose. Reach into the container and take out a bag. Don't look at the bag yet! Close your eyes and open the bag, stick your nose in, and take a deep breath. Make an observation like an expert; "I smell a hint of lavender... and toejam!"

Step 5 Stick your nose back into the bag, deeper this time, and with your facedown in the bag, open your eyes and look through the bag at the outside printed label. It should take only a moment to see which bag you are holding (and so whose sock is in it). Lift your head out of the bag, tilting it back with extra effect and eyes closed as you say, "It's a bouquet that is undeniably . . . Dave!" Hand the first bag back. Grab a second bag and repeat the process.

Step 6 For the last two bags do it this way: Take both bags out and open them. Go back and forth sniffing each, taking a peek at the printed labels just like before. Once you know whose is whose, hand them back to their respective owners. The "feat" ("feet," get it?) is complete!

LOL Joke
Q. Why do cows wear bells?
A. Because their horns don't work.

Super Silly Joke
Q. Why was the boy sitting on his watch?
A. Because he wanted to be on time.

Las Vegas Louie

After explaining that your Uncle Louie is a professional gambler out in Las Vegas, show your friend how he taught you to guess who will win the World Series using a stack of baseball cards. After you each take turns deciding who would win among the teams, your friend is left holding one card. Show your friend the postcard you got from Louie just last week. On the back is a note from Louie: "Kid, I know you like baseball, so I'm giving you a hot tip: Bet on the Phillies!"

What You Need:
- An odd number of baseball cards, each for a different team (You can buy a pack of baseball cards at your local toy store. You should have a pretty big pile—between 15 and 25 is perfect. Remember: The bigger the number, the more impressive it will be that you knew which one would be selected. Be sure to count the baseball cards. The trick only works if you start with an odd number of cards.)
- The Las Vegas Louie Postcard (template on page 139). You'll need to write in your Uncle Louie's prediction for one of the teams on your baseball cards.

How to do it:

Step 1 Sit your friend down and show him the front of the postcard. Tell him that Uncle Louie is a professional gambler, and offer to show your friend how Louie picks out which team will win the World Series. Spread out the cards on the table, and explain the rules.

Step 2 Explain the game like this: "Here's how we play—one person picks two teams (cards). The other person gets to decide which team would win and eliminate the loser. We each take turns matching up teams and deciding who will win. That way, we each have control half of the time. To make it really fair, why don't you decide the first winner for the first matchup? Sounds fair right? Well it's not—that's the cool part!

A

Write your prediction on the back, but show only the front to your friend.

B

Spread out all of the baseball cards, and explain how the game is played.

Step 3 Here are the secret rules you have to remember to make sure that the team you predicted wins the World Series every time: You start by picking the first two teams, so don't pick the team you predicted. That way, whichever team your friend decides to eliminate, it's okay with you. When it's your friend's turn, if one of the teams he picks is the predicted team, you pick the other one (duh!). That's it! After a couple of rounds you will find that your friend is pointing at two teams: the predicted team and one other. Guess which one you choose?

Step 4 Turn Uncle Louie's postcard over, and show your friend that Uncle Louie knew the winner all the time!

C

I KNOW the PHILLIES MUST WIN, SO I'll PICK the OTHER team to LOSE...

In the first round, you pick the two teams, and your friend picks the winner.

D

I PICK PHILLIES to WIN!

In the last round, you pick the winner— it matches your prediction!

Super Silly Joke
Q. How do you make a fire with two sticks?
A. Make sure one's a match.

LOL Joke
Q. What do envelopes say when you lick them?
A. Nothing, it shuts them up!

More Las Vegas Louie!

Extra Stuff to Know and think about:

This "Choose Two, Eliminate One" game can be done with any set of objects. What about inventing another trick, where you predict the Grammy for best new album? Or strongest superhero? Tastiest flavor of ice cream? Notice the phrase "To make it really fair." This is a good one to remember as a magician. You can use this saying in other tricks when you want to make your audience feel that you're not cheating them, even when you really are.

Stretching Your Arm

Startle your friends by making them think you can pull your arm out of its socket!

What You Need:

- A single-serving, half-liter drink bottle made with thin, brittle, clear plastic (You may need to experiment with several brands before you find the bottle that works best for you.)
- Two arms (preferably your own)
- To make this stunt work right, you need to be wearing a long-sleeved jacket or coat

Pre-performance prep:
Before you perform this stunt, practice it in stages in front of a mirror.

Practice stage one:
1. Stick your arms out in front of you. Slowly push your shoulders forward to stick your arms out farther, and then reverse the process; pull your shoulders back so your arms don't stick out as much.

Practice stage two:
1. Stick your arms out, with one shoulder back and the other shoulder forward. Hey! Your arms are different lengths!

2. Now with the hand of your longer arm, grab your other hand and pretend to pull it while you let your shoulder move forward. Hey, your arm stretches!

How to do it:

Step 1 When no one is looking, stick the plastic bottle under your left arm, inside your jacket. You want to get the bottle right in your armpit—the same place you would put your hand if you were going to make a farting noise.

A

Step 2 When you're ready, turn to your friends and exclaim, "Look, I slept on my left arm last night and I think it shrunk!" Stick your arms out, with your right shoulder forward and your left shoulder back.

B

Step 3 Wait a moment so everyone can see the difference in the length of your arms, and then reach across and grab your left hand. With a yank, move your left shoulder forward while you push your arm against your body to crush the bottle. The cracking of the plastic bottle, plus the sight of your arm suddenly stretching, should send at least one friend running for the school nurse!

Step 4 Hold your arms out to show they are now the same length (but don't let the bottle drop)!

Amazing Fact
Your bones can actually stretch! Bones are four times more stretchable than concrete.

LOL Joke
Q. How do you stop a dog barking in the back seat of a car?
A. Put him in the front seat.

Doesn't That Hurt?

• • • • • • • • • • • • • • • • • • • ★ •

Is this classic magic? It's snot!
A perfect trick to show a nosy aunt who's
always trying to pinch your cheeks!
When she asks to see one of your
"cute little magic tricks," take your magic
wand and slowly slide it up your nose!
Don't worry, it's perfectly safe—as long
as she doesn't fall on you when
she faints!

What You Need:

- A vanishing wand (from your local toy or magic store)

How to do it:

Step 1 Hold the wand as shown in figure
A, with your right hand holding the sliding
tip at the bottom and your left hand
holding the other end at the top. (Switch
hands if you're left-handed.)

Step 2 Raise the wand up to your nose, and completely cover the white tip at the top with your left hand. Your hand should look as if it's guiding the wand into your nostril.

Step 3 Tilt the wand so that it matches the angle of your right arm, and then slowly slide the tip up with your right hand. Make sure to hold on to the top of the wand with your left hand. Remember—the wand doesn't go up your nose at all; it just looks as if it does!

Step 4 After you slide the tip about two-thirds up the wand, slide it back down to its original position, and show its full length. Ta-da!

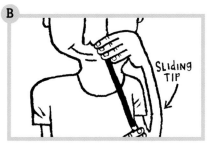

B

SLiding
TIP

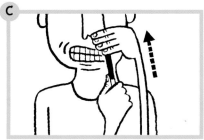

C

Extra stuff to know and think about:

Depending on the length of your arm, you may find it easier to do this trick if you start with the sliding tip a little way up from the bottom. Also, don't worry about getting the sliding tip all the way up to the other end of the wand; just going a couple of inches makes the trick look realistic enough.

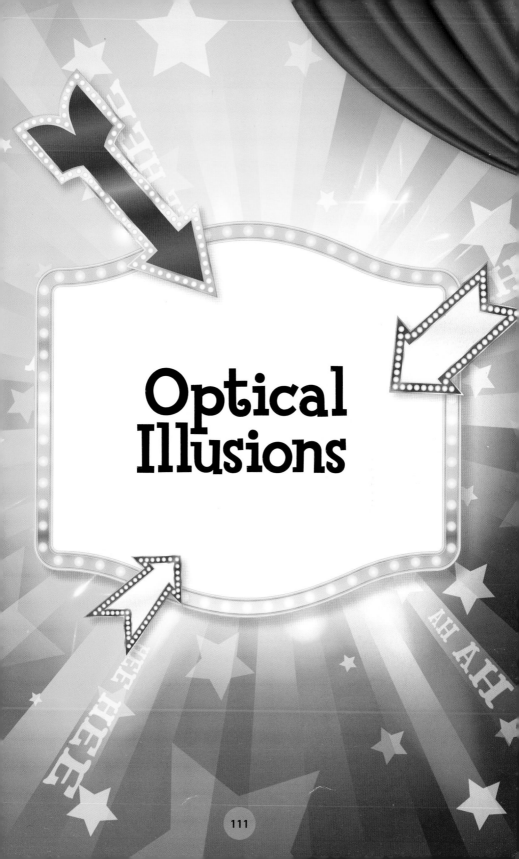

Optical Illusions

Hanky Panky

A handkerchief trick or two, or even several, is part of every magician's performance. And now, at last, you can find out how this old classic is performed.

What You Need:
- A small handkerchief

How to do it:

A

Step 1 Take the handkerchief, and after crushing it into a small ball, tuck it into a fold in your right jacket sleeve at the bend of the elbow, as shown in figure A.

Step 2 Open the hand to show it is completely empty.

B

Step 3 Now turn the hand so that it is back toward the spectators, as shown in figure B and very quickly shoot the hand forward toward the spectators. The handkerchief will make a sudden appearance!

Tips from the Pros
With a little practice, the arm pointing down as you shoot it forward will make the handkerchief land on the hand. You may have to grab it to prevent it from falling on the floor.

Dotty Spots

This trick makes little spots appear mysteriously on the blade of a plastic knife, with just a neat little hand movement.

What You Need:
- A plastic knife
- Some dot stickers (from your local office-supply store)

How to do it:

Step 1 First you must learn the little sleight of hand required for this trick. Hold the knife by the handle in your right hand, so that it is pointing at the floor. Now raise the knife up until it is pointing at the ceiling, but as you raise it upwards, roll the handle of the knife between the finger and thumb, by pushing the thumb to your left.

Step 2 Now reverse the action so that the knife is pointing at the floor, rolling the handle to the right as you do so. It looks as if you have shown both sides of the blade, but in fact, you have shown the same side of the blade twice. This is the basis of the effect.

Step 3 To prepare this trick, place three dot stickers on one side of the blade. Have another three dots handy.

Step 4 Now show the blank blade, and then "show" the other blank side of the blade.

Step 5 Now take another dot sticker, and place it on the side that has no dots. Now lift the knife to show that there is another dot on the other side of the blade. By doing our secret move, you are in fact showing the same spot twice.

Step 6 Place a second dot on the blade. Now show that a second dot has appeared on the other side, as before. Now add a third dot, and show that a third dot has appeared. Now hand them the knife to let them see that there really are six spots on the knife.

Amazing Fact
Harry Houdini's real name was Erich Weiss.

Super Silly Joke
Q. What did zero say to eight?
A. Nice belt.

LOL Joke
Two goldfish are in a tank. One of them turns to the other and says, "How do you drive this thing?"

Not-so-Solid Glass

The impression in this trick is that you are pushing your magic wand right through the bottom of a glass. To prove the glass is quite genuine, tap its bottom inside and out several times, with a bit of a flourish. Suddenly, as you are doing this, the wand appears to penetrate the bottom of the glass. For a brief moment the spectators think they see the wand sticking out through the bottom of the glass.

What You Need:
- A wand (from your local toy or magic store)
- A glass

How to do it:
Step 1 Hold the glass in your left hand, and push the wand into the glass so that it hits the bottom, as shown in figure A.

Step 2 Remove the wand. Turn the glass over, and hit the outside bottom of the glass.

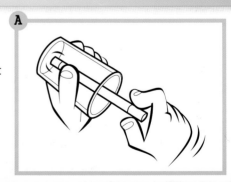

A

Step 3 After hitting the bottom of the glass several times, inside and out, push the wand behind the glass, slipping it between the glass and the palm of your left hand. Push the wand further, so it seems to pass through the bottom of the glass, as shown in figure B.

Step 4 Now withdraw the wand instantly, and look quizzically at the bottom of the glass, as if you're not quite sure what happened.

B

Tips from the Pros
The whole sequence should be done quickly, as a sort of throwaway item; perhaps as a prelude to a trick in which the glass is used.

LOL Joke
Q. Why did the computer go to the doctor?
A. Because it had a virus.

Amazing Fact
If you're "double-jointed," it doesn't mean that you have two joints where most people only have one—it actually means that you can stretch your ligaments.

The Wobbly Wand

This is an odd one. It is not exactly a magic trick, but an optical illusion, which can be used to make spectators think that you have strange powers. In it, a solid wand wobbles as if it were rubber.

What You Need:
- A wand (from your local toy or magic store) or a pencil

How to do it:

Step 1 Hold the wand as shown in figure A. Grip it loosely between the finger and thumb. Hold the wand up at the eye level of your admiring audience.

A

Step 2 Now move the hand up and down in a straight line for a distance of about 4 inches. Do it slowly at first, and gradually speed it up until the end of the wand begins to wave up and down and appear to be soft and bendy.

Tips from the Pros
Try it a few times to know what speed to shake the wand. Then there is no need to start slowly. Once mastered, do it with pencils, pens, swizzle sticks, wooden rulers, etc.

Touchy, Touchy

You've got fingertips that were made for cracking safes! Your friends hand you a penny, a dime, and a nickel behind your back; you correctly "feel" the date on each and every one without ever bringing your hand in front of your body!

What You Need:

- A nickel, a dime, and a penny (None of them should be particularly new or old.)

This one is sooo easy—and so cool—that the hardest part will be not giggling when you do it. It's most effective right after you leave the convenience store, when you know your friends have a pocket full of change.

Pre-performance prep:

Memorize the dates of the three coins. Remember: You need to memorize the dates and which type of coin has each date. Put the three coins in your back pocket.

How to do it:

Step 1 Explain to your friends that you have trained your fingertips to be super sensitive. Ask your friends if they have any change. When they start looking, put your hands behind your back. With one hand, reach into your back pocket and grab the three coins. Hold them loosely, but close your hand enough to hide the coins. When your friends find their money, dramatically turn your head and say, "No, no, I don't want to see."

Step 2 Turn your back. Put your other hand behind you, and ask your friends to put a nickel, a dime, and penny into your hand. Once you have the coins, turn around with your hands still behind you, and casually drop these coins into your other back pocket.

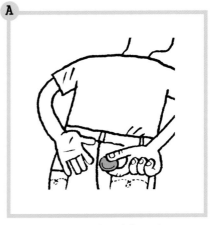

Turn around, and show the coins to your friends.

Step 3 From now on it's all acting! Use both hands to feel all three of your coins. Because of the difference in size, it will be easy to tell which is which. Pick out the penny and say, "Because of my extraordinary sense of touch, I know that I'm holding the penny!" Your friends will not be impressed. You continue, "On the back it says 'One Cent,' and on the front it says 'In God We Trust.'" Your friends will point out that all pennies do. Then you hit them with the punch line: "This particular penny has a date. The date is . . . 1 . . . 9 . . . 7 . . . 2: Nineteen-seventy-two!"

Step 4 Instead of bringing your hand in front of your body, make a big deal about turning around and holding the coin out for someone to check the date. This way the coins are never in front of your body. Turn your back again. "I will now read the dates on the other two coins. Notice that the other two coins remain behind my back the whole time." Now after the proper acting of "feeling the coins" announce the dates of the dime and the nickel. Bring these coins out and have the dates checked. The trick is complete!

B

FIXed COINS

Hold your coins in one hand, and drop the others into your back pocket.

Super Silly Joke
Q. Why do fish live in salt water?
A. Because pepper makes them sneeze.

More Touchy, Touchy

Extra stuff to know and think about:

Notice that you don't tell your friends what you are going to do before you start. If you did, they might decide to look at the dates on the coins before they gave them to you. Then what would you do? Most of the time it's best not to tell your audience exactly what you are attempting before you start. If you do, they'll stop watching what you're doing and start thinking about how you're going to fool them. This makes your job much harder.

Duh! Don't be a dummy and ask for the coins back! Remember that everyone thinks those coins are the ones you borrowed. Try this trick: Once you memorize the dates, start checking your change for more coins that have the same dates. For example, if you start with a dime from 1975, start collecting dimes from this date. That way you will have a ready supply of coins, and you won't have to remember new dates every time you do the trick.

Amazing Fact
When gambling was outlawed in 18th-century England, every casino had an employee whose only job was to swallow the dice if the authorities showed up.

LOL Joke

Q. What is black, white, and red all over?

A. A sunburnt penguin.

Super Silly Joke

Q. Where did the sheep go on vacation?

A. The Baaaaahamas.

LOL Joke

Q. How do Eskimos make their beds?

A. With sheets of ice and blankets of snow.

Squishy Spheres

How do you make three spheres out of two? Your friend will not only be amazed when you try this trick, she'll actually help you do it!

What You Need:

- Squishy spheres (from your local toy or magic store)

Pre-performance prep:

You'll need to practice "palming" the squishy spheres to make this trick work. Start by placing one in the palm of your hand and covering it with your thumb. Try to squeeze the ball tightly, and then practice turning your hand over and moving it around (without dropping the sphere). Once you've mastered palming one, try palming two spheres in the same hand.

How to do it:

Step 1 First palm a sphere in your left hand. Tell your friend that you need her help finding a missing piece of your magic kit. Then pick up the other two spheres with your right hand.

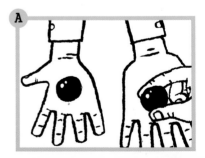

B

Step 2 Ask your friend to hold out her hands; place one sphere in each hand. Then ask her how many of the squishy spheres she sees (and don't be surprised if she looks at you like you've suddenly lost your marbles). She'll probably say, "Two."

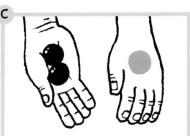

C

Step 3 Shout, "Eureka! You've found it!" and reach behind her ear. Quickly pull the third sphere out from behind her ear with your left hand. You've done the trick!

Cash Rebate

Always trying to squeeze more out of your allowance?
Take a close look at it and announce,
"Yup, this one is still full."
When your friend asks what you
mean, you roll the dollar into a tube
and dump out some change.

What You Need:
- Three dimes
- Phony thumb, also called a "thumb tip" (from your local toy or magic store)

How to do it:

Step 1 Before you start, squeeze the thumb tip, as shown in figure A, and slide in the dimes. You should have plenty of room to shove your thumb into it.

Step 2 With the phony thumb in place, ask to borrow a dollar. If this is difficult, offer to show your friends with one of your own dollars. Hold the dollar as shown.

Step 3 Say, "This is just a dollar; no more, no less!" and show your empty hands one at a time, like this: Let go of the dollar with your left hand and show your empty hand, front and back. Position your hand with your fingers open and your thumb facing your friends. Re-grip the dollar with your left hand, and let go with the right. Show your empty right hand, front and back, and then re-grip the dollar.

Step 4 Turn the dollar, and wrap it around the fake thumb from front to back into a tube. Re-grip the wrapped dollar with your left hand, and pull your right thumb out of the thumb tip. You may need to push the thumb tip into the tube a little bit just to make sure the edge doesn't show.

Step 5 Hold your right hand flat, and squeeze the thumb tip with your left hand as you dump the coins out. Tilt the tube so that no one gets a look inside. Stick your thumb back into the tube and unroll the dollar, ending with the dollar between your hands.

Step 6 Hold the bill with your right hand, and lay it down while you pick up the 30 cents with your left hand. Put the coins into your right hand, and drop them in your front pocket. Casually pull out your hand, leaving the thumb behind. Your friends will never know what hit 'em!

Fake THUMB

Extra stuff to know and think about:

If your friends are watching really closely, don't be in a rush to put the thumb away. If you suddenly plunge your hands into your pockets right after you finish the last step of the trick, everyone will be suspicious. If you want, display the bill and your hands again after you unroll the bill. Trust me—they can stare, but since they don't know what they're looking for, they won't see anything! The thumb tip helps you perform amazing magic, but it won't work if you tell even ONE of your friends (believe me, they'll talk). Keep this a complete secret!

Magician's Tip

Moving your body one part at a time is called an "isolation." Body isolations are used by performers all the time, but mostly by dancers (especially break dancers) and mimes.

Visited by Aliens

Tell one of your buds about your close encounter with an alien named b801. The alien helps you by reading people's minds. Your bud thinks up a big number. You take him through some Martian math, and he ends up with an even bigger number—a number he didn't know he would choose; a number you can't possibly know. But your intergalactic partner sends you the answer!

What You Need:
- The b801 Alien Card (template on page 141)
- A pencil and paper for your friend

How to do it:

Step 1 Take out the b801 Alien Card, and tell your friend that you recently met an alien who told you that aliens are controlling the thoughts of humans.

Step 2 Tell your friend to think of a three-digit number, where all the digits are different. If he asks why, tell him, "Because it makes it harder for the alien to control your thoughts."

Step 3 Tell your pal to reverse the digits of the original number, and then subtract the smaller number from the larger one. Remind him to make sure to do the math correctly because "you don't want to mess up the translation." See figure A.

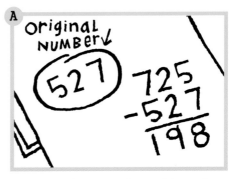

Reverse the chosen number, and then subtract whichever one is smaller.

Extra stuff to know and think about:

This is what magicians call a "force." A force happens anytime you make your audience think they have a free choice, but you're actually forcing them to pick the thing you want. (See page 30 for another trick that uses a force).

Step 4 Now have your friend take this new number and reverse the digits. Then add the two numbers together. (Note: If the number is 99, have him add a zero when he reverses it, so that he changes 99 to 990.)

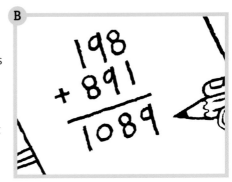

Reverse the result,
and add the two numbers together.

Step 5 Remind your friend that there's no way for you to know his original number, the number he came up with once he did the subtraction or the new number after he did the addition. Then ask him what his final number is.

Step 6 Take out the Alien Card again, and explain that your extraterrestrial buddy is obviously sending you a message using your friend's brain as the envelope! Say, "b801 made you think of his name!" Place the pad upside down next to the card, and show your friend that he has indeed written the alien's name!

C

Compare the b801 Alien Card
with the upside-down math.
They match!

NAME: B801
SPECIES: LUMBATION
ANTENNAE LENGTH: 1.5 FEET
RESIDENT PLANET: NEPTUNE
SPACESHIP LICENSE NO.: STRGAZN

A Magical World

So there you go—our favorite gross and twisted tricks, which are bound to leave your friends staring at you with their mouths open so wide that they should worry about swallowing flies.

So what's next? Well, first go back and learn all the tricks you skipped because they looked too hard, were too long to read, or seemed too scary to perform. (Wondering how I knew you skipped a couple? I'm a magician—I know everything!)

Now get out there and start performing. Magic is like riding a bike: When you first start, you spend a lot of your time looking at the ground, trying not to mess up or fall on your face. But the fun really starts when you get good enough to forget about pedaling and steering and you start looking around. If you go out and do these tricks a lot, soon you'll feel comfortable enough to relax and look around too. You'll start seeing ways to improve the stories you tell—or even to improve the tricks themselves. You'll start thinking of really funny things to say. Most important, you'll have a chance to see how your audience reacts. And that's where the magic really takes place—on the faces and in the imaginations of your audience.

Remember to have fun and be confident, and you'll become a skilled magician in no time!

Having trouble finding some of the supplies needed to perform the tricks in this book? You can find most of these items laying around the house or at your local hardware or office-supply store. If you still can't find what you need, ask your mom or dad to take you to a toy or magic store— you'll definitely find what you're looking for.

Go Forth & Amaze

Once you've mastered all of the tricks in this book, you'll be well on your way to being a real magician, and amazing your friends at the same time!

If you're a beginner, pick a few of the easier tricks and learn them first. Three or four tricks are enough to amaze your friends in a casual setting. The Next Card (#2), Watch That Ring (#39), and The Wobbly Wand (#90) make a great combination. For a short performance, only one or two more tricks are needed. If you know in advance, you can prepare a longer, more difficult sequence, like the following: When Is a Cut Not a Cut? (#47), A Knotty Problem (#49), Where Is It Now? (#59), and The "Under 21" Prediction (#29). Save the tricks that take a lot of preparation for special occasions. The easier ones are the ones you do when someone says, "Hey, you're a magician. Show us a trick."

So go forth and amaze, magicians! All you need is some skill and confidence and you'll be surprising and making people laugh in no time!

Giant Ten of Diamonds Card

Photocopy and use with the trick on page 26.
(Don't forget the back side!)

Las Vegas Louie Postcard

Photocopy and use with the trick on page 100.
(Don't forget the back side!)

Place
Stamp
Here

To: